# COOPER'S PACK™

## ALASKA

by kyle & groot

Cooper's Pack Publishing

*Cooper's Pack® - Alaska* is a work of fiction. Any resemblance to real people or animals, stuffed or otherwise, is purely coincidental.

All the animals had fun in the writing of this book.



ISBN-13: 978-0-9794882-3-8
ISBN-10: 0-9794882-3-0

Library of Congress
Control Number: 2011900008



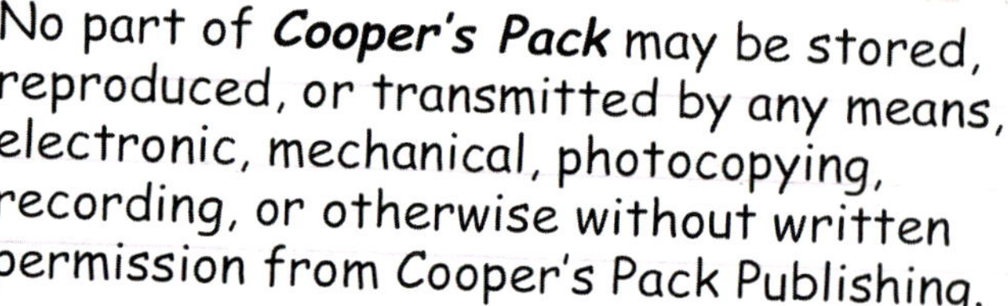



For user permissions, onsite visits, or additional information, visit www.cooperspack.com or contact us at cooper@cooperspack.com or 877-278-3278.

Electronic version available online at the App Store.

Distributed by PGW through ORO editions
www.pgw.com

Printed in China by ORO Group Ltd

Airlines
Nationality
USA
Passport C
01506
Given Name
COOPER
Date of Birth
JUN 19
Place of birth
WASHINGTON, USA
Issued On
31 DEC 09
C0150619420
UNITED STATES DEPARTMENT OF
COOPER
MVP Gold ******15
BOARDING PASS
To
Juneau
Flight From
Seattle
MOUNT ROBERTS®
TRAMWAY
Juneau, Alaska
WHITE PASS & YUKON ROUTE
Since 1898
Special
Excursion Ticket
Trip Passage
Date: 05/20
Passenger: COOPER
non-transferable
From/To
JNU SGY
Ticket# 5450930
IT# 1653053
ARS SGY11-011
ALASKA
CANOPY ADVENTURES

I've always wanted to go.
I guess I should go.
There is no reason not to go.
Game on, here I go!
...***north to Alaska***!

Plotting my course.

Flying fish anyone?

De-bark-ation time.

I purchased my ticket to Alaska, America's 49th state, land of the midnight sun.

I packed my bags and was off for the last frontier!

I landed in ***Juneau*** and took a bus downtown.

Although I did my research on Juneau, a smart traveler always knows to talk to a local for the best information.

Juneau is the state capital and third largest city in Alaska. The city is only accessible by plane or boat.

I saw a friendly moose selling tours so I walked over to get some information.
"Welcome to Juneau," said the moose. "Folks call me Kodi."
"Hi Kodi, I'm Cooper. Can you help with some ideas to see the sights?"
A friendly moose.
TRIP EACH WAY
WHEN IN NOME
We Offer
Whale Watching
Helicopter
Glacier Trek
Float Planes
Zip Lining
Dog Sledding
City Trolley Tours $19
Trolley Tours $19 45 min.
Trolley City Tour $19 45 min tour
$7 GLACIER TRIP EACH WAY
City Trolley Tours $19
PRIVATE WHALE WATCHING
City / Glacier Tours
EVERY 30 MINUTES
Glacier Shuttle $7 Each Way
WHILE SUPPLIES LAST!
ULTIMATE ALASKA ADVENTURE
OFFICIAL ANTLER CAP
ULTIMATE ALASKA ADVENTURE
1 nhall Shuttle $7 Ea. Way
2 Mendenhall Glacier / City Tour $27 2.5 hr.
3 City Trolley Tours $19 45 min.

"If you are looking for the best, greatest, coolest tour ever, the ***Ultimate Alaska Adventure*** is for you."

How could I say no?

I paid for the tour and we immediately set off for the ***Mount Roberts Tramway***.
Turns out Kodi was going to be my guide.
How cool is that?
BERTS TRAMWAY
POOCH PASS
TOUR INFORMATION
TICKETING
TRAMWAY ENTRANCE
My personal guide.
OPEN
OFFSEASON MOOSE ENTRANCE
OTTER TODAY
OTTER TODAY

The Tramway rises 1,745 feet (541 meters) from the base and travels at 23 miles per hour.

Kodi took me to a lookout spot and we surveyed the town below.

"Not to worry, Coop, we don't have to walk down," Kodi said with a smile.

After taking the Tram back down the mountain, Kodi took me on a walking tour of downtown Juneau.

"Tell me about your guide business," I asked.

"I have the best job in the world," Kodi told me. "I get to meet new people every day, during the season anyway."

"The season?"

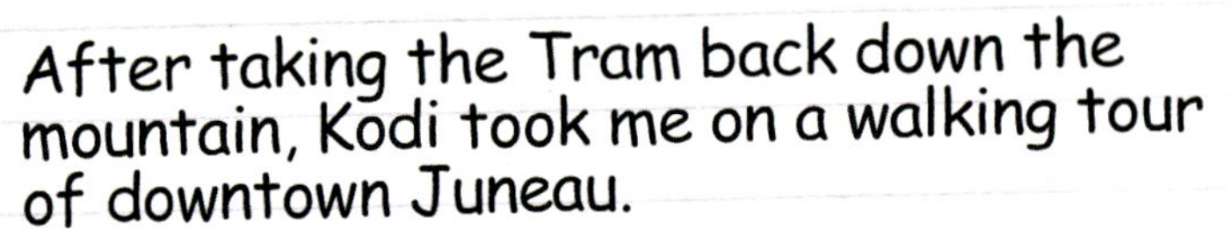

Hitting the pavement.

Nice doggy...

What do they mean "no miners"?

"Most visitors come to Alaska during the summer months when the cruise ships arrive and the weather is nicer," he explained. "The tourist season."

We ended up down on the waterfront in front of a large ship.

"Almost all of the ships come up from Seattle, Washington and Vancouver, Canada," Kodi explained.

"From the dock, they look like giant buildings," I said.

Indeed they do.

A building with lifeboats?

Almost half of all visitors to Alaska arrive via cruise ship.

Kodi asked, "Are you ready to see something bigger than all of the cruise ships combined?"

"You know it!"

"We're going to go see the ***Mendenhall Glacier***," Kodi said as he put on a scarf.

After a short drive from downtown Juneau, we arrived at Mendenhall Glacier. The glacier was humongous, crazy large, gigantic. It seemed to go on forever.

"I've never seen anything like this!" I exclaimed.

Iceberg ahoy...

Mendenhall Glacier was formed during the Little Ice Age, about 3,000 years ago. It is 12 miles long, up to 1.5 miles wide.

Bluest. Blue. Ever.

Kodi explained how Mendenhall Glacier is retreating into the mountains, which is another way to say it is melting.

"The icebergs you see are bits of the glacier that break off into the lake."

"Bits indeed."

"You haven't seen anything yet," Kodi added. "Wait until we walk on it!"

We left the glacier base and arrived at a helicopter pad.

After securing our seatbelts, we were off to see it from above.

How cool is that!?!

"From the air it looks like a river of ice," I said.

"That's because it is."

Deep, spooky crevasses...

Crunch, crunch, crunch...

I had to admit, Kodi ran a great tour.

Landing up on the glacier and feeling the crackle of ice under my feet is one of the coolest things I have ever done.

Period.

The Orange Boar
COMING SOON
After returning to downtown Juneau, I thanked Kodi for the great tour.
"Oh it's not over yet, kiddo. I'll pick you up at your hotel tomorrow morning. Get ready for day two of your Ultimate Alaska Adventure."

With a smile on my face, I headed to get a quick souvenir and checked in for the night.

What a great day!

Kodi picked me up the next morning and we boarded a tiny prop plane. We were off on Day #2 of my Ultimate Alaska Adventure.

"Where to, Captain Kodi?"

"North to ***Skagway***!" he replied.

The front seat rocks!

Skagway, Alaska

As we approached Skagway, Kodi explained our mission.

"We're here to learn about the ***Klondike Gold Rush***, plus it is a fun town to explore."

Fun and exploring? Two of my favorite activities...

"Game on!"

Skagway was small enough that we could actually walk from the airport into downtown...it only took 3 minutes!
"What makes Skagway so special?" I inquired.
SKAGWAY HARDWARE CO.
SPORTING GOODS
MEGA MOOSE VITAMINS
DEDMAN'S
"Much of the great Klondike gold rush began here in Skagway," Kodi explained. "Prospectors came from around the world to find gold in the hills and this was the starting point."
Formerly called Skagua (schlag-wah) which is a Tlingit name for "home of the wind". Turns out it is quite windy in Skagway.

"In the old days they had to hike 500-plus miles into the Yukon Territory. Today we can simply take the train to see what their journey was like."
AB
A B
CAMP SKAGWAY No 1
1899

We headed over to the ***White Pass & Yukon Route*** Railroad depot and purchased two tickets to ride the rails.

UAA
We boarded the train and were off to see Alaska's interior and the border with Canada.

The train took us out of Skagway—up into the mountains, through tunnels, and across several bridges.

The views were breathtaking, especially on the narrow tracks overlooking the valley below.

The *WP&YR* climbs up almost 3,000 feet in just 20 miles. Originally 110-miles long, today it travels only the first 67.5 miles stopping at Carcross, Yukon.

"Remember," Kodi added, "before the train, people used to have to hike this route or take the ***Chilkoot Trail***. Either way, they were required to carry over 1 ton (2,000 pounds) of supplies, mostly food, to survive the long winters."

Off to the Yukon...

I could only imagine what it must have been like.

Gold sure makes people work hard!

"Speaking of, let's go see some gold for ourselves," Kodi said.

Panning for a poke…

To learn more about the gold rush, we headed out to the ***Klondike Gold Fields***.

The ***Dredge*** as it is called, features many exhibits and artifacts, plus you can actually pan for gold!

Mush, mush...you mush!

The Dredge also includes a tour featuring dogsled puppies who are in training for Alaska's great ***Iditarod*** race.

The Iditarod is the longest dog sled race in the world, traversing across Alaska for over 1000 miles each year.

We decided to walk back into town and stopped off at a secret waterfall behind the ***Gold Rush Cemetery***.
CHOOSE YOUR TRAIL
Street Car
Cemetery
Wm Nash Died June 1,1898
Chadwick BIGGS Died Apr. 28 1898
Jack Bordok Died 1898
Glad I wasn't here in 1898.
"You're quite the tour guide," I told Kodi. "Where did you learn about all of these great places?"
Kodi responded, "By traveling, like you."

The day was coming to a close as we entered town.
"Best to grab a quick bite and then we're off to our next destination," Kodi suggested.
KIRMSE'S
CURIOS
MOES FRONTIER BAR
Billboards - old school.

We arrived at the ***Alaska Marine Highway*** ferry terminal.

"C'mon, Coop, we're taking the overnight ferry out of town!"

"Ships and sleep, just what I needed. Sweet!" I replied.

The Alaska Marine Highway consists of a fleet of ferries that transport goods, vehicles, and passengers between Alaska, Canada and Bellingham, Washington.

"You've seen the state capital and you've learned about the quest for gold. Now it's time to see the rest. Get some sleep and when we wake up, we'll be in ***Ketchikan***."

As I dozed away, I dreamt of trains atop gold-covered glaciers...now if I could just get that moose to stop snoring.

After a few stops overnight and the next day, we arrived in Alaska's salmon capital, otherwise known as Ketchikan.

We set out to explore the town and learn about Alaska's 4th largest city.

"Hard to believe the weather, huh Coop?" Kodi said. "Summers in Alaska can be downright hot."

"We could actually wear shorts," I said, laughing at the thought of a traveling moose and a dog wearing shorts.

"Here in Alaska we have trees galore. So much so, timber is one of our major exports...that and fish of course," Kodi said.

"I've got an idea. Let's go see the ***Lumberjack Show***. They'll make you laugh while rooting for your favorite lumberjack team."

POLE CLIMBING

SAWING

CHOPPING

The show features pole climbing contests, log rolling competitions, plus amazing ax and sawing skills.

These folks really know their wood, I thought.

After the show, we wandered over to an area called ***Creek Street***.

The "street" is built up on stilts and sits right over the river.

A fun-icular? Yup, a funicular.

Picture perfect!

"C'mon Coop, let's take the shortcut to the top," Kodi said.

We arrived at the top of the hill and took a short walk down the backside over to the ***Totem Heritage Center***.

This is a great place to learn about totem poles and how the local **Tlingit** Indians built them to tell family stories and legends.

Totem poles!

If you like totem poles, also visit Bight State Historic Park, Saxman Native Village and the Southeast Alaska Discovery Center.

"It's hard to believe but totem poles only last for about 100 years," Kodi said.

"Must be due to using wood," I offered.

"Yeah, but they just make new ones, with new stories and family histories."

Cool.

After making some new totem pole friends, we found ourselves in ***City Park***.

The park was quiet and a great place to simply hang out.

I asked Kodi what his favorite place in Alaska was.
"That's easy, Coop...wherever I am. The people here are always nice and the smiles never get old (except during hunting season of course)."
Sometimes it is tough being a moose.
→ STEDMAN
↑ City Park
↑ Fountain
→ Totem Heri
City Park is the perfect place to have a picnic or run around and play.

Kodi took another shortcut and I met him on the other side. He sure does know his way around...

"Let's hit the waterfront for the grand finale of your Ultimate Alaska Adventure."

"Game on," I said, hoping that eagle didn't think we were snacks.

No trip to Alaska is complete without seeing the ***Misty Fjords*** outside of Ketchikan.

"Do tell?" I asked Kodi.

"Oh, I can't tell you...I can only show you."

"Ta da! Jump in, Coop, and we will be up and away in no time."
A sea plane! How cool is that?
OFFICIAL UAA SEAPLANE
Beaver

We strapped ourselves in and took off from the water.

Sea planes are exactly that--planes that can land and take off from the water.

C-Dog to K-Moo. Over. Roger.

Fjords from afar.

Glacier carving (scarring).

The pilot aimed for the lake below and we swooped in for a landing.

The sea plane came to a stop at a little secret dock in the middle of nowhere.
"Kodi, this really has been the ultimate Alaska adventure. I can't thank you enough for being such a great guide."
"Just wait until your next visit. I'll take you to Mt. McKinley, the Arctic and even Cooper's Landing," Kodi said.
"Next trip?" I said to myself, realizing yes, the next trip. "I can't wait!"

"You are quite the adventurer, Cooper. Know that you will always have a friend here in Alaska, unless it is hunting season when I will be in hiding."

Kodi asked the pilot to fly straight from our hidden lake to the airport.

The tour was over and it was time to go home. I had the best time ever...

Alaska is amazing: the land, the people, the history.
It is bigger than I ever thought possible and actually makes me feel pretty big too (inside).
I realized a trip to Alaska stays with you forever. That makes me smile.

Cooper's Pack Travel Guide to
ALASKA
Juneau · Skagway · Ketchikan
ACTIVITIES
-Outdoor Activities
-Transportation
-A Brief History
-Alaska's Glaciers
-Cooper's Photos
-Biographies
COOPER'S PACK™
TRAVEL GUIDES
by kyle & groot

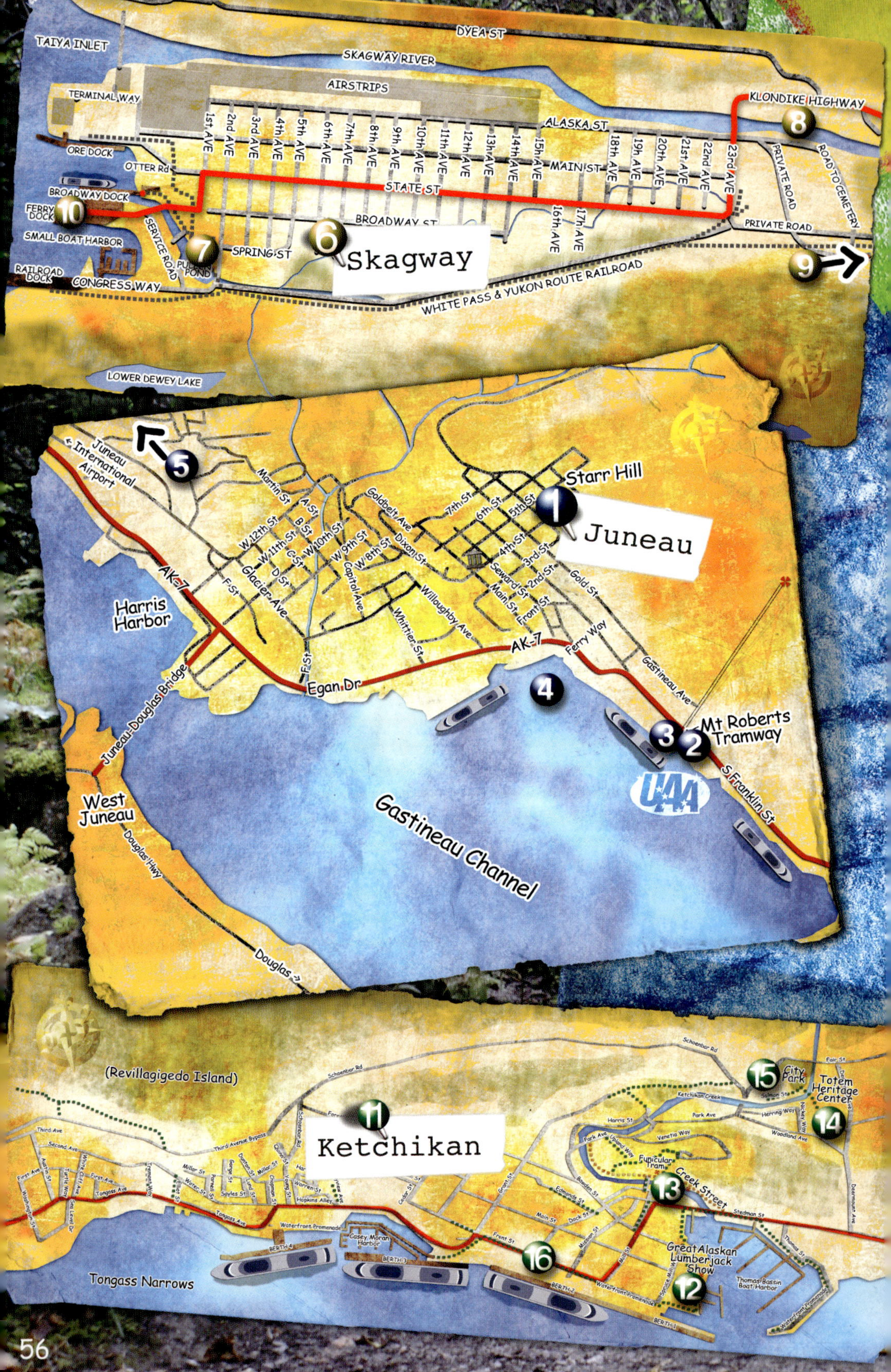

TAIYA INLET
DYEA ST
SKAGWAY RIVER
AIRSTRIPS
TERMINAL WAY
ALASKA ST
KLONDIKE HIGHWAY
ORE DOCK
OTTER Rd
MAIN ST
STATE ST
BROADWAY DOCK
FERRY DOCK
SMALL BOAT HARBOR
RAILROAD DOCK
CONGRESS WAY
SERVICE ROAD
SPRING ST
BROADWAY ST
1st AVE
2nd AVE
3rd AVE
4th AVE
5th AVE
6th AVE
7th AVE
8th AVE
9th AVE
10th AVE
11th AVE
12th AVE
13th AVE
14th AVE
15th AVE
16th AVE
17th AVE
18th AVE
19h AVE
20th AVE
21st AVE
22nd AVE
23rd AVE
PRIVATE ROAD
ROAD TO CEMETERY
Skagway
WHITE PASS & YUKON ROUTE RAILROAD
LOWER DEWEY LAKE
Juneau International Airport
Starr Hill
Juneau
Martin St
A St
B St
C St
D St
F St
W 12th St
W 11th St
W 10th St
W 9th St
W 8th St
Glacier Ave
Capitol Ave
Goldbelt Ave
Dixon St
Willoughby Ave
Whittier St
7th St
6th St
5th St
4th St
3rd St
2nd St
Seward St
Main St
Front St
Gold St
Ferry Way
Gastineau Ave
AK-7
Egan Dr
Harris Harbor
Juneau-Douglas Bridge
Mt Roberts Tramway
S Franklin St
West Juneau
Douglas Hwy
Douglas
Gastineau Channel
(Revillagigedo Island)
Ketchikan
City Park
Totem Heritage Center
Funicular Tram
Creek Street
Great Alaskan Lumberjack Show
Tongass Narrows
Tongass Ave
Waterfront Promenade
Casey Moran Harbor
Thomas Basin Boat Harbor

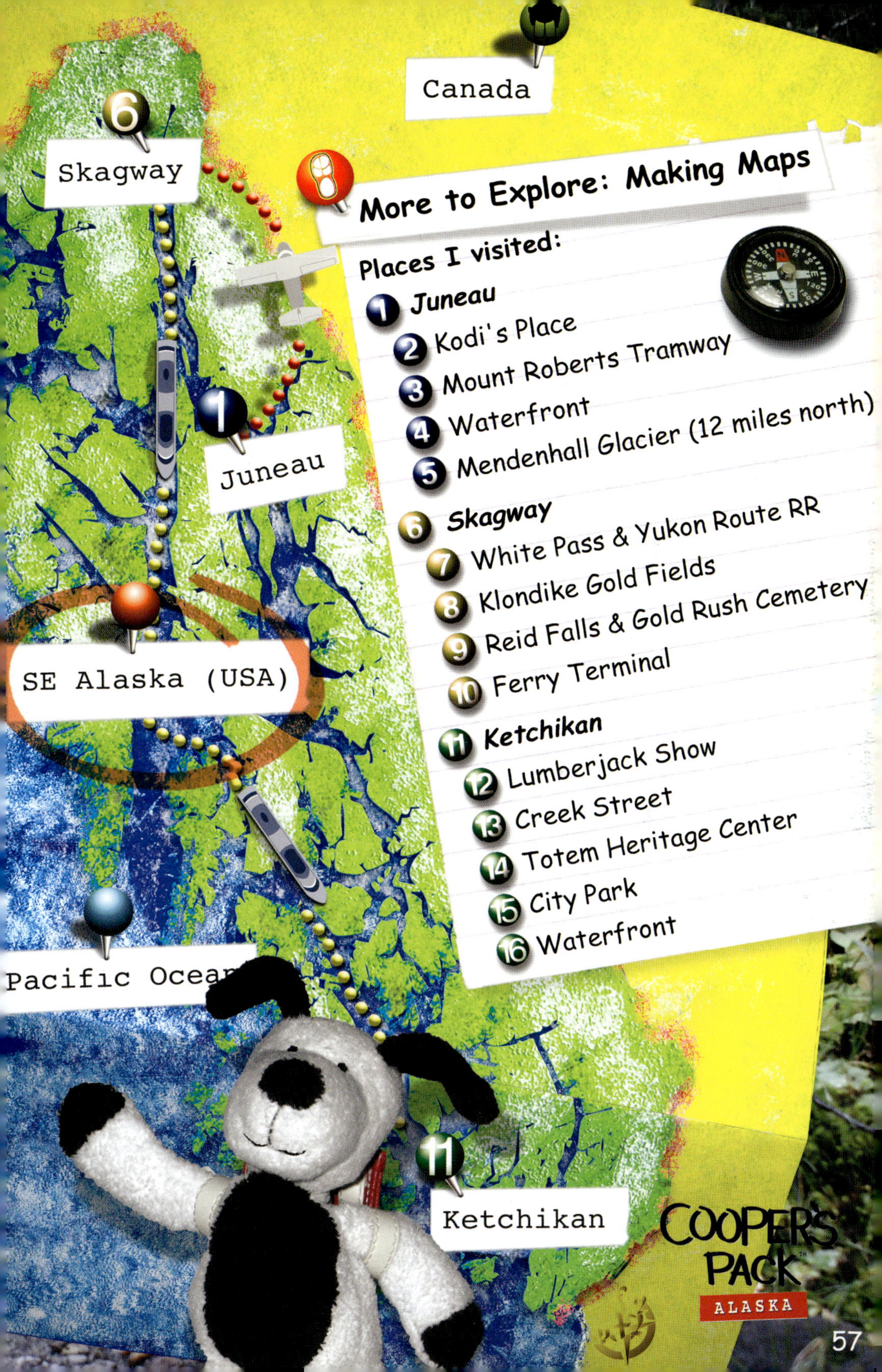
Canada
Skagway
Juneau
SE Alaska (USA)
Pacific Ocean
Ketchikan
More to Explore: Making Maps
Places I visited:
1 Juneau
2 Kodi's Place
3 Mount Roberts Tramway
4 Waterfront
5 Mendenhall Glacier (12 miles north)
6 Skagway
7 White Pass & Yukon Route RR
8 Klondike Gold Fields
9 Reid Falls & Gold Rush Cemetery
10 Ferry Terminal
11 Ketchikan
12 Lumberjack Show
13 Creek Street
14 Totem Heritage Center
15 City Park
16 Waterfront
COOPER'S PACK
ALASKA

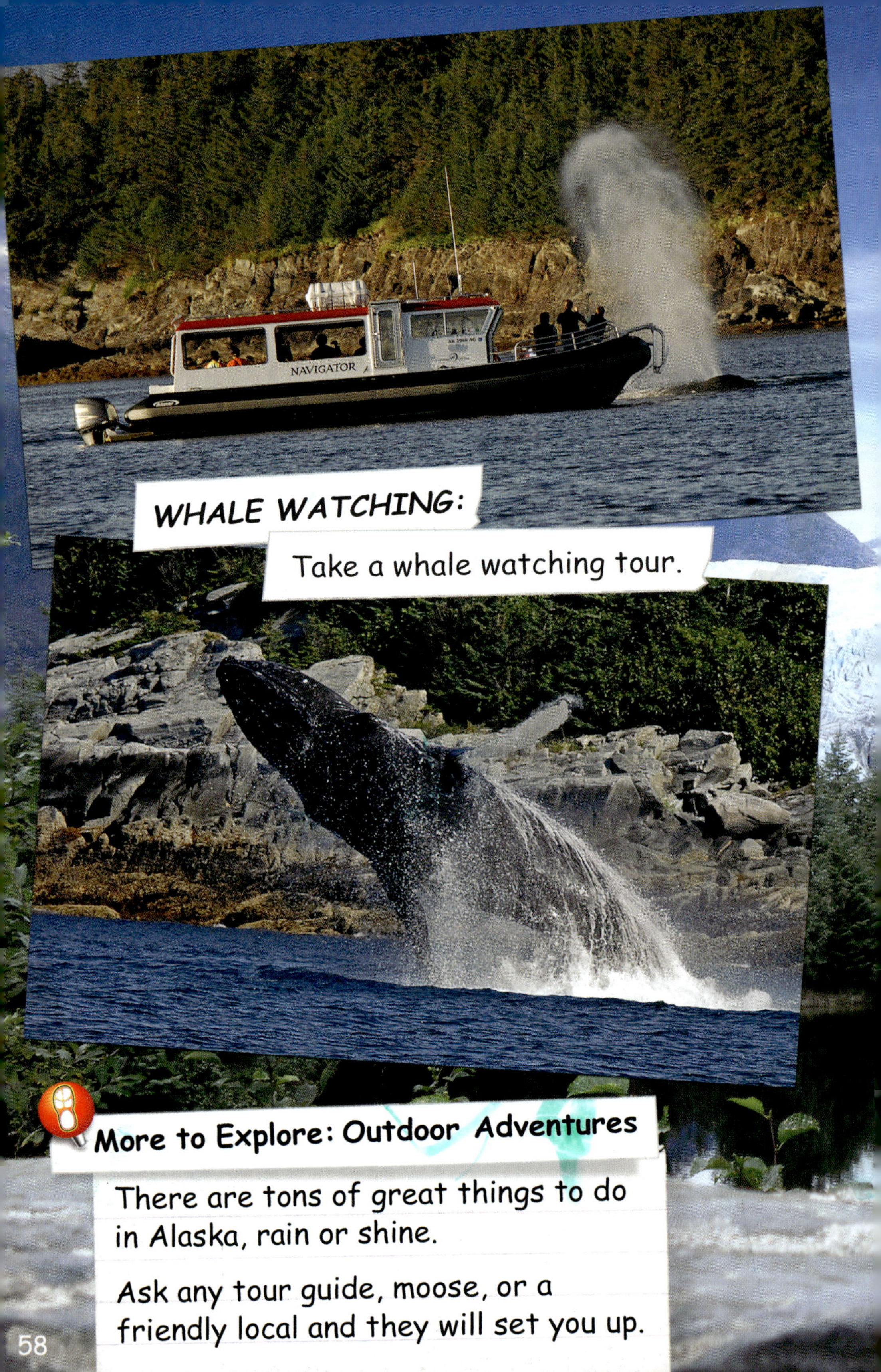


## WHALE WATCHING:

Take a whale watching tour.

## More to Explore: Outdoor Adventures

There are tons of great things to do in Alaska, rain or shine.

Ask any tour guide, moose, or a friendly local and they will set you up.

ZIP LINES:
Zip through the forest, the fun way...
VISIT A GLACIER:
Helicopters make it easy...
TEMSCO
N57958
COOPER'S PACK™
ALASKA

Serious 4x4.

High-speed ferry.

Ducks in Ketchikan.

Hard to miss the cruise ships...

**More to Explore: Transportation**

How do you travel within Alaska?

There are many ways to get around...

Helicopters rule!
Tour boats abound.
ADVENTURE BOUND
KYLE01
GROOT1
Sea planes are like bicycles in Alaska.
RED ONION SALOON
SKAGWAY ALASKA STREET CAR TOUR
ALL POINTS OF INTEREST
WORLD
Streetcar tours.
COOPER'S PACK
ALASKA

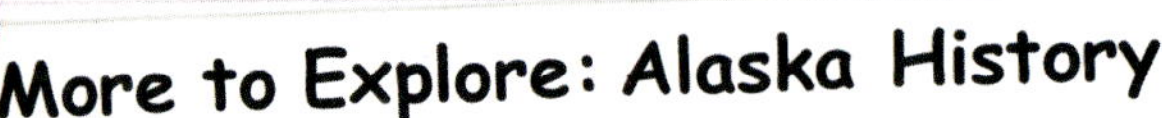


Alaska was purchased from Russia in 1867 for $7.2 million (about 2 cents an acre). At the time, most Americans thought this was a waste of money. Considering Alaska's vast natural resources including oil, natural gas, gold, fish and timber, it turned out to be the deal of the century.

Way to go, William Seward!

Alaska became the 49th state in 1959 and is the largest in the U.S., measuring 586,400 square miles. It is so big that you could cut it in half and it would be the TWO largest states.

GOLD RUSH
SLED DOGS

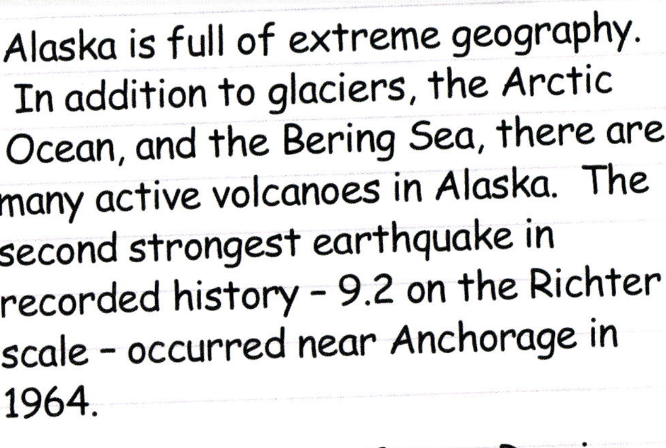

Alaska is full of extreme geography. In addition to glaciers, the Arctic Ocean, and the Bering Sea, there are many active volcanoes in Alaska. The second strongest earthquake in recorded history - 9.2 on the Richter scale - occurred near Anchorage in 1964.

Alaska's name came from a Russian version of the Aleut word Alakshak, meaning great lands or peninsula.

Dog mushing is Alaska's state sport and the state mammal is the moose (we knew you were special, Kodi!).

Alaska is called Land of the Midnight Sun. In the most northern parts of the state, the sun does not set at all from May to July!

The Native People of Alaska are Eskimos (two main groups, Inupiat and Yupik), American Indians (Athabaskan in the central part of Alaska and the Tlingit, Tsimshian and Haida in the southeast) and Aleuts (native to the Aleutian Islands and other parts of south and west Alaska).

After Hawaii, the next two largest islands in the U.S. are in Alaska - Kodiak and Prince of Wales.

Located in Denali National Park, Mt. McKinley (also called Denali meaning "the high one") is the highest mountain in North America (20,320 ft. / 6,194 meters). As well as its scenery, the park is famous for wildlife viewing which includes grizzly bears, moose and caribou.

The largest bears in the world are found in Alaska (the Kodiak bear and the polar bear—measuring up to 11 feet tall).

Alaska is only 55 miles from Russia (mainland to mainland).

The state flag was designed by a 13-year old named Benny Benson. Well done, Benny!

## More to Explore: Alaska's Glaciers

Thousands of glaciers have helped to form Alaska's landscape for over 115,000 years. Glaciers are found throughout areas of Alaska, with many easily accessible from ***Anchorage*** and ***Juneau***. A glacier is like a river, but made of compacted snow and ice. They are formed in places with heavy snow yet temperatures that do not melt them in the summer.

Most are receding (getting smaller) yet there are a few including ***Hubbard Glacier*** that are advancing (getting bigger). Glaciers can end at the sea (tidewater glaciers) or at a lake (freshwater glaciers). Some simply end in a valley (called valley glaciers).

You will often see dark blue ice within a glacier. This means it is very dense and old.

Icebergs are made from pieces of a glacier that separate (calve) and fall into a lake or the sea.

Whether seen from a boat, plane, helicopter, or even your car, the memories will last a lifetime.

Some famous Alaska glaciers include:
• Columbia Glacier (near Valdez)
• Glacier Bay National Park (near Juneau)
• Hubbard Glacier (Shared with Canada)
• Mendenhall Glacier (Juneau)
• Childs Glacier (Cordova)
• Exit Glacier (Seward)
COOPER'S PACK™
ALASKA

WP&YR Engine 73.

The writing's on the wall at the Dredge in Skagway.

En route south from *Skagway*.

**More to Explore: Cooper's Photos**

Remember to take a camera when you visit Alaska!

Nothing misty here...
Cardinal
COOPER FOR GOVERNOR
Dogs in Ketchikan are cooler than most...
Juneau
Co-Captains Cooper and Kodi.
COOPER'S PACK™
ALASKA

# COOPER

**Eye Color:** Black
**Born:** Olympic Mountains (outside of Seattle, WA)
**Home:** Bainbridge Island

**Favorites:**

**Foods:** T-bone Steak, Milk
**Color:** Navy blue
**Places:** Hiking, Pacific Ocean, Grandpa's house
**Books:** A Separate Peace
**Artist:** Marcus Bausch, Jr.
**Teacher:** Mr. Axling (Geography)
**Class:** Geography, Languages
**Music:** Tragically Hip, Beatles
**Sports:** Soccer, Skiing, Boating
**Hobbies:** Traveling, Writing
**Sayings:** "Top Dog", "You rock!"
**Nicknames:** Coop

# Kodi

**Eye Color:** Brown
**Born:** Kodiak, Alaska
(Kodiak Archipelago)
**Home:** Juneau, Alaska

**Favorites:**
**Foods:** All Things Vegetarian,
Gummi Bears
**Color:** Camouflage
**Places:** Glacier Bay, Kodiak Island
**Books:** Animal Farm
**Artist:** Rie Muñoz, Wassily Kandinsky
**Teacher:** Mr. See
**Class:** Calculus, Cartography
**Music:** Pink Floyd, James Brown
**Sports:** Snowshoeing, Dogsledding
**Hobbies:** Hiking, Playing Guitar
**Sayings:** "I'll get you there"
**Nickname:** K-Moo, the Flying Moose

Name:

Height:

Weight:

Eye Color:

Born:

Languages:

**Favorites:**

Places:

Books:

Music:

Sayings:

Nickname:

**Travel Information:**

Date: ______________________________

Destination(s): ______________________________

______________________________

______________________________

______________________________

Transportation: ______________________________

______________________________

______________________________

______________________________

______________________________

Don't forget to add your own drawings.

COOPER'S PACK™ ALASKA

Send Cooper your travel stories, highlights and photos of your stuffed animal friend(s) to: **Cooper@CoopersPack.com**

You may find them featured on Cooper's website, including updates and additional pictures of Cooper's adventures.


## Credits / Acknowledgements:

Tamala & Daren Booton
Michael Tripp
Carol DeMatteis
Ryan Chesla (Page 4)
White Pass & Yukon Route RR
Klondike Gold Fields
Gold Rush Sled Dog Tours (page 31)
Temsco Helicopters
Alaskan Canopy Adventures
Gastineau Guiding Company
Jim Hammond (page 58)
Rie Muñoz
Mount Roberts Tramway
Alaska Airlines
Great Alaskan Lumberjack Show
Totem Heritage Center
Tongass Trading Company
Kodi's Ultimate Alaska Adventure
Tony Newell
Victoria Wellman
All of the great people Cooper met in Alaska

**kyle**

Likes to play his guitar.

**groot**

Would love to play the piano.